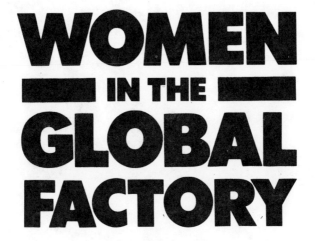

WOMEN
— IN THE —
GLOBAL
FACTORY

BY
ANNETTE FUENTES &
BARBARA EHRENREICH

INC PAMPHLET NO. 2
EDITORS: HOLLY SKLAR & GLORIA JACOBS
COPY EDITOR: MADELON BEDELL
DESIGNER: CYNTHIA CARR

SOUTH END PRESS

Cover photo: Electronic assembler, El Salvador.
Photo by Women and the Global Assembly Line Project

Fourth printing, March 1987

Copyright © 1983 Institute for New Communications

ISBN 0-89608-198-2

The following people provided essential ideas, criticisms and encouragement during the creation of this pamphlet: Linda Gail Arrigo, John Cavanagh, Lynn Duggan, Maria Patricia Fernandez Kelly, Maria Luisa Rivera and Lisa Schnall.

Production of this pamphlet was assisted by a grant from an anonymous donor, on the recommendation of Joint Foundation Support. An earlier version of part of this material appeared in *Ms.* magazine as "Women on the Global Assembly Line" (January 1981), written by Barbara Ehrenreich and Annette Fuentes.

TABLE OF CONTENTS

LIST OF TABLES AND BOXES

SONG OF THE FACTORY GIRLS

Oh, sing me the song of the Factory Girl!
So merry and glad and free!
The bloom in her cheeks, of
   health how it speaks,
Oh! a happy creature is she!
She tends the loom, she watches
   the spindle,
And cheerfully toileth away,
Amid the din of wheels, how her
   bright eyes kindle,
And her bosom is ever gay.

Source: Publication subsidized by textile mill owners in the 1840s.

AROUND THE WORLD WITH MULTINATIONAL CORPORATIONS

In Penang, Malaysia, Julie K. is up before the three other young women with whom she shares a room and starts heating the leftover rice from last night's supper. She looks good in the company's green-trimmed uniform and she's proud to work in a modern, U.S.-owned factory. Not quite so proud as when she started working three years ago, she thinks, as she squints out the door at a passing group of women. All day at work, she peers through a microscope, bonding hair-thin gold wires to silicon chips that will end up inside pocket calculators. At 21 years of age, she is afraid she can no longer see very clearly.

In the 1800s, farm girls in England and the northeastern United States filled the textile mills of the first Industrial Revolution. Today, from Penang to Ciudad Juarez, young Third World women have become the new "factory girls," providing a vast pool of cheap labor for globetrotting corporations. Behind the labels "Made in Taiwan" and "Assembled in Haiti" may be one of the most strategic blocs of womanpower of the 1980s. In the last 15 years, multinational corporations, such as Sears Roebuck and General Electric, have come to rely on women around the world to keep labor costs down and profits up. Women are the unseen assemblers of consumer goods such as toys and designer jeans, as well as the hardware of today's "Microprocessor Revolution."

Low wages are the main reason companies move to the Third World. A female assembly line worker in the U.S. is likely to earn between $3.10 and $5 an hour. In many Third World countries a woman doing the same work will earn $3 to $5 a *day.* Corporate executives,with their eyes glued to the bottom line, wonder why they should pay someone in Massachusetts on an hourly basis what someone in the Philippines will earn in a day. And, for that matter, why pay a male worker anywhere to do what a female worker can be hired to do for 40 to 60 percent less?

U.S. corporations call their international production facilities "offshore sourcing." To unions these are "runaway shops" that take jobs away from American workers. Economists, meanwhile, talk about a "new international division of labor," in which low-skilled, labor-intensive jobs are shifted to the "newly industrializing" Third World countries. Control over management and technology, however, remains at company headquarters in "First World" countries like the U.S. and Japan. In 1967, George Ball, senior managing director of Lehman Brothers Kuhn Loeb (an international investment company) and a former undersecretary of state, described the phenomenon this way:

Today a large and rapidly expanding roster of companies is engaged in taking the raw materials produced in one group of

countries, transforming these into manufactured goods with the labor and plant facilities of another group, and selling the products in still a third group. And, with the benefit of instant communications, quick transport, computers and modern managerial techniques, they are redeploying resources and altering patterns of production and distribution month to month in response to changes in price and availability of labor and materials.[1]

The pace of multinational production has accelerated rapidly since the mid-1960s. The electronics industry provides a good example of the new international division of labor: circuits are printed on silicon wafers and tested in California; then the wafers are shipped to Asia for the labor-intensive process in which they are cut into tiny chips and bonded to circuit boards; final assembly into products such as calculators, video games or military equipment usually takes place in the United States. Yet many American consumers don't realize that the goods they buy may have made a

Your Payroll dollars are 50% more productive in Puerto Rico than the total U.S. average.

At an American Hospital Supply Corp. subsidiary, Teresa Rodriguez inspects a multi-flanged ventricular catheter designed to aid in hydrocephalus shunt procedures for the human brain. Teresa is one of 60,000 high-tech workers in Puerto Rico.

In Puerto Rico, U.S.A. the value added per dollar of production payroll averages $5.58 compared to the U.S. average of $3.72.*

How do we ~~~~ |

in 1982 our average wage including fringe benefits was $6.02. On the mainland it was $11.62.*

Our people adapt easily to high-tech manufacturing. They're ~~

almost 93% of the top three management positions in the 2,500 manu-facturing operations here are held by Puerto Rican ~~~

global journey, and represent the labor of people in several countries—or that the "foreign" products that worry U.S. workers may have been made in factories owned, at least in part, by U.S. corporations.

History of the Global Factory

The Multinational Corporation. The Sun Never Sets On It...The profit motive has propelled it on a fantastic journey in search of new opportunities.

Irving Trust Company advertisement

In a 1971 survey, "low wage rate" was the main reason corporations gave for choosing offshore sites.[2] Fairchild Camera and Instrument Corporation was among the earliest to expand overseas; in 1961 it established an export production plant in Hong Kong where wages were about 28 cents an hour. More and more firms followed suit. Corporate executives rationalized their decision in terms of growing international competition: "Our major customer had bids from the Japanese and from American companies with offshore plants. We had to go abroad to compete."[3]

Multinationals spread quickly in the 1960s, first to Hong Kong and Taiwan, next to South Korea and Mexico and then Singapore and Malaysia, seeking ever cheaper production bases for the assembly of everything from baseballs to washing machines. From 1960 to 1969 investment in offshore manufacturing by U.S. firms mushroomed from $11.1 billion to $29.5 billion.[4] In the mid-seventies Thailand and the Philippines became corporate favorites. The assembly line was stretching.

By moving overseas, corporations were able to escape U.S. and European trade union demands for more stringent health and safety standards as well as higher wages and benefits. The public's growing concern with industrial pollution could be neatly sidestepped by transferring the pollution to countries that had no environmental regulations. As a Malaysian Health Ministry doctor explained, "The government's policy is to attract investors. The first question

CHEAP LABOR
WAGES PER HOUR IN U.S. DOLLARS

	Wage	Wage & Fringe Benefits
Hong Kong	$1.15	$1.20
Singapore	.79	1.25
South Korea	.63	2.00
Taiwan	.53	.80
Malaysia	.48	.60
Philippines	.48	.50
Indonesia	.19	.35

Source: *Semiconductor International*, February 1982.

an investor asks is: 'What regulations do you have, and how well do you enforce them?' If he finds these two areas are weak, he comes in."[5]

During this period, earlier Third World economic development strategies—emphasizing the promotion of national industry and decreased dependence on imports from the U.S. and other Western countries—were scrapped for a new approach that, not coincidently, fit the needs of multinational corporations. By 1965, export-led industrialization had become the favored strategy for development, touted by the United Nations Industrial Development Organization (UNIDO), the World Bank and the International Monetary Fund (IMF), along with multinational corporations and banks. Third World countries were to roll out the red carpet for foreign investors and become "export platforms" producing goods for the world market. In return, "host governments" were promised jobs, technology and foreign exchange (earnings in such international currencies as the dollar and mark which are necessary for the purchase of imports such as oil and machinery). With assistance from UNIDO and the U.S. Agency for International Development (AID), "developing countries" designed their economies according to the multinational corporate blueprint. Protective trade barriers, of the kind used to protect U.S. and British industry in their fledgling years, were dropped to permit the "free flow" of capital and goods across national boundaries. Foreign investors were assured the full repatriation of their profits and Third World governments outdid each other offering tax incentives. For companies that preferred not to own and operate factories offshore,

subcontracting arrangements with local firms were encouraged as an alternative.

Free Trade Zones

Free trade zones (or export processing zones, as they are also known) have emerged as key elements in this export-led development. The free trade zone is a haven for foreign investment, complete with electricity and other infrastructure and a labor force often housed in nearby dormitories. It is a colonial-style economic order, tailormade for multinational corporations. Customs-free import of raw materials, components and equipment, tax holidays of up to 20 years and government subsidization of operating costs are some of the enticements to investment. National firms are usually prohibited from operating in the zones unless they invest jointly with a foreign company.

Free trade zones—there are now over 100—mean more freedom for business and less freedom for people. Inside, behind walls often topped with barbed wire, the zones resemble a huge labor camp where trade unions, strikes and freedom of movement are severely limited, if not forbidden. A special police force is on hand to search people and vehicles entering or leaving the zones.

According to a highly-placed Third World woman within the United Nations, "The multinationals like to say they're contributing to development, but they come into our countries for one thing—cheap labor. If the labor stops being so cheap, they can move on. So how can you call that development? It depends on the people being poor and staying poor."

Puerto Rico's "Operation Bootstrap" which began in the late 1940s, was a preview of the free trade zone model of "development." The Puerto Rican Economic Development Administration placed an advertisement in U.S. newspapers in 1976, appealing for corporate investment with the promise "You're in good company in Puerto Rico, U.S.A." where there are "higher productivity, lower wages and tax-free profits." But companies aren't necessarily good for Puerto Rico. Under "Operation Bootstrap" export production increased as production of domestic necessities declined. In 1982, unemployment topped 30 percent; the island of Puerto Rico, with its tropical climate and fertile soil, now imports almost all of its food as well as manufactured goods from the "mainland."[6] To pay for these costly imports, the country has gone into debt to U.S. banks and other lending agencies. In 1976, when the initial tax "holidays" for foreign investors ran out and minimum wage laws were implemented, many companies left to exploit even cheaper labor in Haiti and the Dominican Republic.

Women on the Global Assembly Line

We need female workers; older than 17, younger than 30; single and without children; minimum education primary school, maximum education one year of preparatory school [high school]; available for all shifts.

Advertisement from a Mexican newspaper

A nimble veteran seamstress, Miss Altagracia eventually began to earn as much as $5.75 a day..."I was exceeding my piecework quota by a lot."...But then, Altagracia said, her plant supervisor, a Cuban emigre, called her into his office. "He said I was doing a fine job, but that I and some other of the women were making too much money, and he was being forced to lower what we earned for each piece we sewed." On the best days, she now can clear barely $3, she said. "I was earning less, so I started working six and seven days a week. But I was tired and I could not work as fast as before." Within a few months she was too ill to work at all.

Story of 23-year-old Basilia Altagracia,
a seamstress in the Dominican Republic's
La Romana free trade zone,
in the *AFL-CIO American Federationist.*[7]

There are over one million people employed in industrial free trade zones in the Third World. Millions more work outside the zones in multinational-controlled plants and domestically-owned subcontracting factories. Eighty to ninety percent of the light-assembly workers are women. This is a remarkable switch from earlier patterns of foreign-controlled industrialization. Until recently, economic development involved heavy industries such as mining and construction and usually meant more jobs for men and—compared to traditional agricultural society—a diminished economic status for women. But multinationals consider light-assembly work, whether the product is Barbie dolls or computer components, to be women's work.

Women everywhere are paid lower wages than men. Since multinationals go overseas to reduce labor costs, women are the natural choice for assembly jobs. Wage-earning opportunities for women are limited and women are considered only supplementary income earners for their families. Management uses this secondary status to pay women less than men and justify layoffs during slow periods, claiming that women don't need to work and will probably quit to get married anyway.

Women are the preferred workforce for other reasons. Multinationals want a workforce that is docile, easily manipulated and willing to do boring, repetitive assembly work. Women, they claim, are the perfect employees, with their "natural patience" and

Haiti

Women and the Global Assembly Line Project

"manual dexterity." As the personnel manager of an assembly plant in Taiwan says, "Young male workers are too restless and impatient to be doing monotonous work with no career value. If displeased they sabotage the machines and even threaten the foreman. But girls, at most they cry a little."[8]

Multinationals prefer single women with no children and no plans to have any. Pregnancy tests are routinely given to potential employees to avoid the issue of maternity benefits. In India, a woman textile worker reports that "they do take unmarried women but they prefer women who have had an operation," referring to her government's sterilization program.[9] In the Philippines' Bataan Export Processing Zone the Mattel toy company offers prizes to workers who undergo sterilization.[10]

Third World women haven't always been a ready workforce. Until two decades ago, young women were vital to the rural economy in many countries. They worked in the home, in agriculture, or in local cottage industries. But many Third World governments adopted development plans favoring large-scale industry and agribusiness as advocated by such agencies as the World Bank and the International Monetary Fund. Traditional farming systems and communities are now crumbling as many families lose their land and local enterprises collapse. As a result of the breakdown of the rural economy, many families now send their daughters to the cities or the free trade zones in an attempt to assure some income.

The majority of the new female workforce is young, between 16 and 25 years old. As one management consultant explains, "when seniority rises, wages rise;" so the companies prefer to train a fresh group of teenagers rather than give experienced women higher pay. Different industries have different age and skill standards. The youngest workers, usually under 23 years old, are found in electronics and textile factories where keen eyesight and dexterity are essential. A second, older group of women work in industries like food processing where nimble fingers and perfect vision aren't required. Conditions in these factories are particularly bad. Multinationals can get away with more because the women generally can't find jobs elsewhere.

Not all companies want young women, although this is the exception rather than the rule. In Singapore, some companies had problems with young women workers who went "shopping for jobs from factory to factory." Management consultants suggested "housewives-only" assembly lines. Older and too responsible for "transient glamour jobs," housewives would make better candidates, they reasoned. One consultant recommended that "a brigade of housewives could run the factory from 8 a.m. to 1 p.m.

Lynn Duggan

Ricoh watch factory, The Philippines

and leave. Then a second brigade could come in [and] take over till 6 p.m. This way housewives need only work half a day. They will be able to earn and spend time with their families. The factories will get a full and longer day's work. Deadlines will be met."[11]

Corporate apologists are quick to insist that Third World women are absolutely thrilled with their newfound employment opportunities. "You should watch these kids going to work," said Bill Mitchell, an American who solicits U.S. business for the Burmudez Industrial Park in Cuidad Juarez. "You don't have any sullenness here. They smile." A top-level management consultant who advises U.S. companies on where to relocate their factories said, "The girls genuinely enjoy themselves. They're away from their families. They have spending money. They can buy motor bikes, whatever. Of course, it is a regulated experience, too—with dormitories to live in—so it's a heathful experience." Richard Meier, a professor of environmental design believes that "earning power should do more for the women of these countries than any amount of organization, demonstration and protest...The benefits and freedom to be gained by these women from their employment in these new industries are almost always preferred to the near slavery associated with the production of classical goods, such as batik."[12]

Liberation or virtual slavery? What is the real experience of Third World women? A study of Brazilian women working in a textile factory drew positive conclusions: work "represents the widening of horizons, a means of confronting life, a source of individualization. The majority of women...drew a significant part of their identity from being wage-workers."[13] By earning money and working outside the home, factory women may find a certain independence from their families. Meeting and working with other women lays the foundation for a collective spirit and, perhaps, collective action.

But at the same time, the factory system relies upon and reinforces the power of men in the traditional patriarchal family to control women. Cynthia Enloe, a sociologist who organized an international conference of women textile workers in 1982, says that in the Third World, "the emphasis on family is absolutely crucial to management strategy. Both old-time firms and multinationals use the family to reproduce and control workers. Even recruitment is a family process. Women don't just go out independently to find jobs: it's a matter of fathers, brothers and husbands making women available after getting reassurances from the companies. Discipline becomes a family matter since, in most cases, women turn their paychecks over to their parents. Factory life is, in general, constrained and defined by the family life cycle."

One thing is certain: when multinational corporate-style development meets traditional patriarchal culture, women's lives are bound to change. ●

EAST ASIA: THE "ORIENTAL GIRLS"

The manual dexterity of the Oriental female is famous the world over. Her hands are small, and she works fast with extreme care...Who, therefore, could be better qualified by nature and inheritance, to contribute to the efficiency of a bench-assembly production line than the Oriental girl?

Malaysian government investment brochure

I've sold five years of my youth to the company. I need a rest from this brain-numbing work for two or three weeks. But there is no way I can leave without quitting or taking a big loss. There are so many regulations you feel you are tied up with ropes till you can't budge an inch. And I've given them five years of my life!

Taiwanese factory worker[14]

Half a million East Asian women are estimated to be working in export processing zones. Women are heavily employed in export manufacture outside the zones as well. In South Korea women between 16 and 25 years of age comprise one-third of the industrial labor force.[15] A great percentage of these "factory girls" come from rural areas, drawn to the burgeoning urban centers by reports from friends or older sisters who've landed an assembly job. When there isn't a large enough pool of would-be factory workers in the cities, companies go out recruiting in the countryside, often enlisting the help of village authorities and the fathers and brothers of factory-age women. In Taiwan, large companies work with junior high school principals who offer up busloads of recent graduates to labor - hungry plants.[16] For the majority of women, it is their first job experience. They may even be the first wage - earners in their families.

While some women live close enough to factories to remain with their families and commute by bus, most workers are forced to find accomodations near the plant. Housing is scarce and expensive for their meager wages. In Malaysia, researcher Rachel Grossman of the Institute for Labor Education and Research found women employees of a U.S. company living four to eight in a room in boarding houses, or squeezed into tiny extensions built onto squatter huts near the factories. Access to clean water is often non-existent or severely limited. Where companies do provide dormitories for their employees, they are not of the "healthful" collegiate variety described in corporate propaganda. Dormitory rooms are small and crowded, with beds shared by as many as three shifts of workers: as one worker gets up to go to the factory, another returning from work takes her place in bed. As many as 20 women may be crammed into a tiny space. In Thailand, staff members of the American Friends Service Committee (AFSC) found filthy dormitories with workers forced to improvise a place to sleep among splintered floorboards, rusting sheets of metal and scraps of dirty cloth.

The great majority of the women earn subsistence-level incomes, whether they work for a multinational corporation or a locally-owned factory. While corporate executives insist that their wages are ample in view of lower standards of living, the minimum wage in most East Asian countries comes nowhere near to covering

Women walking to work, Taiwan

Linda Gail Arrigo

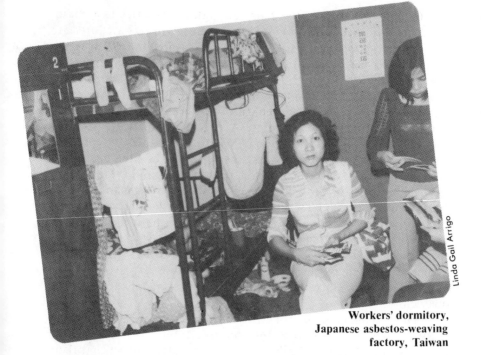

Linda Gail Arrigo

**Workers' dormitory,
Japanese asbestos-weaving
factory, Taiwan**

basic living costs. In the Philippines, starting wages in U.S.-owned electronics plants are between $34 and $46 a month; the basic cost of living is $37 a month for one person. In Indonesia, the starting wages are about $7 less per month than the básic cost of living.[17] And that basic cost of living means bare subsistence: a diet of rice, some dried fish and water, lodging in a small room occupied by four or more people.

Contrary to corporate belief, most women don't use their wages to buy motor bikes and personal luxury items. A much-advertised Coke is a "luxury" that might cost half a day's wage. Meager as their wages are, however, most women are important wage earners for their families. A 1970 study of young women factory workers in Hong Kong showed that 88 percent were turning more than half their earnings over to their parents. In Malaysia, women electronics workers contribute 25 to 60 percent of their wages to their families.[18] And there is a growing pressure on women of both farm and lower-income urban backgrounds to postpone marriage and find work to help out their families.

Health Hazards
Subsistence wages are only part of the picture. Most women work under conditions that can break their health or shatter their

nerves within a few years, often before they've worked long enough to earn more than a subsistence wage.

Consider first the electronics industry, which is generally thought to be the safest and cleanest of the export industries. Inside the low, modern factory buildings, rows of young women, neatly dressed in company uniforms or T-shirts, work quietly at their stations. There is air conditioning, not for the women's comfort, but to protect the delicate semiconductor parts they work with. High-volume popular music is piped in to prevent talking. Electronics is near the top of the list, prepared by the U.S. National Institute on Occupational Safety and Health (NIOSH), of high health-risk industries. Open containers of dangerous carcinogenic acids and solvents, giving off toxic fumes, are commonplace in electronics factories. In a Hong Kong clinic survey of workers who use chemicals, 48 percent had constant headaches, 39 percent were often drowsy and 36 percent had frequent sore throats.[19]

Anthropologist Linda Gail Arrigo was in Taiwan when 12 women died from inhaling toxic fumes at a Philco-Ford plant. "One 18-year-old woman was stricken after only three weeks on the job," she said. "The company claimed she had a mysterious hereditary disease. After the news of those cases got out, the company gave her parents $2,500—less than half of her medical bills for a slow, painful death."

At one stage of the assembly process, workers have to dip the

Japanese asbestos-weaving factory, Taiwan

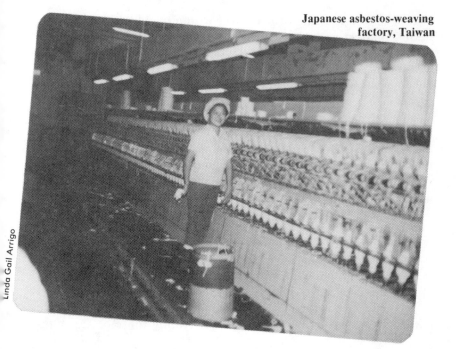

Linda Gail Arrigo

"SAEMAUL SPIRIT"

In South Korea, Confucian values of loyalty and devotion to parents are being redirected toward industry by the Saemaum Pondsadan, a business organization which has formed groups at 980 industrial firms; its steering committee is made up of 37 leading companies in the country.

Companies in the Saemaum Pondsadan select exemplary workers to attend four-day seminars at Saemaul Education Centers. Seminars include a series of lectures on the "Saemaul spirit," illustrated by a movie featuring a Korean factory girl who achieves financial security by being thrifty and working overtime. Seminar participants are expected to bring the Saemaul spirit of devotion and self-sacrifice back to their factories. "Saemaul girls" arrive at work early to perform volunteer tasks like cleaning the factory and sweeping the street outside, try to reduce errors and waste in production and are expected to be available for work during breaks and lunch time without demanding extra pay.

Source: Christina Tse, *The Invisible Control: Management Control of Workers in a U.S. Electronic Company,* Center for the Progress of Peoples, Hong Kong, 1981.

circuits into open vats of acid. According to AFSC staffpersons Irene Johnson and Carol Bragg, who toured a National Semiconductor plant in Penang, Malaysia, women who do the dipping wear rubber gloves and boots. But these sometimes leak and burns are common. It is not uncommon for whole fingers to be lost in the process.

Electronics companies require perfect vision in new employees, but most women need glasses after a few years on the job. During the bonding process women peer through microscopes for seven to nine hours a day attaching hair-like gold wires to silicon chips. One study in South Korea found that most electronics assembly workers developed eye problems after only one year of employment: 88 percent had chronic conjunctivitis; 47 percent became nearsighted; 19 percent developed astigmatism.[20] The companies treat these health complaints with indifference. "These girls are used to working with the scopes. We've found no eye problems. But it sure makes me dizzy to look through those things," said a plant manager at Hewlett-Packard's Malaysia operation.[21]

Unlike electronics factories, conditions in the garment and textile industry are visibly unhealthy, rivaling those of any 19th-

Leah Margulies and Holly Sklar, "Women and Global Corporations" slide show

century sweatshop. The firms, generally local subcontractors to large U.S. (and European) chains such as J.C. Penney and Sears, show little concern for the health of their employees. Some of the worst conditions have been documented in South Korea, where the garment and textile industry helped spark that country's so-called "economic miracle." Workers are packed into poorly lit rooms, where summer temperatures rise above 100 degrees Fahrenheit. Textile dust and lint, which can cause brown-lung disease, fill the air. The dampness that is so useful in preserving thread, causes rheumatism and arthritis among the workers.

In her diary (originally published in a magazine which has since been banned by the South Korean government) Min Chong Suk, a sewing-machine operator, wrote of working from 7 a.m. to 11:30 p.m. in a garment factory:

> When [the apprentices] shake the waste threads from the clothes, the whole room fills with dust and it is hard to breathe. Since we've been working in such dusty air, there have been increasing numbers of people getting tuberculosis, bronchitis, and eye disease...it makes us so sad when we have pale, unhealthy, wrinkled faces like dried-up spinach ...It seems to me that no one knows our blood dissolves into the threads and seams, with sighs and sorrows.

"Permanent Casuals"

Women factory workers are in a precarious situation, treated like temporary workers, always under the threat of layoffs. Sick leave, holidays and vacations are almost unheard of. A woman from a distant village risks her job if she takes off for more than the maximum two-or three-day leave to visit her family. A probationary or apprenticeship period of six months or so, during which pay is only three-quarters of the regular wage, is common. By laying off workers just before the end of their probation, companies save the expense of a full wage. Workers are so used to this practice that they refer to themselves as "permanent casuals."

RIPE FOR LABOR AGITATORS?

South Korean factory workers get a free hand-out from their bosses—a book written by Hong Ji Yong, a former member of the Korean Central Intelligence Agency. The book explains why "communists" and religious groups concerned with labor reform "are very much more interested in getting women workers than men workers:"

> First, women are more susceptible than men. They are emotional and less logical. They cannot differentiate between true and false or good and bad...They are easily excited and are very reckless and do things hastily...Third, most women workers are sentimental young girls. Fourth, women workers are so caught by vanity that they spend much more money than men workers... Sixth, management, union leaders and city administrators find it very difficult to deal with women workers when they cause trouble. The women weep and cry and behave exaggeratedly... and for men this kind of behavior is very troubling.

Source: *Connexions*, a feminist quarterly, Fall 1982, p. 15.

Women and the Global Assembly Line Project

Bataan Export Processing Zone, The Philippines

In Taiwan, Hong Kong and Malaysia, a bonus pay system often comprises a large part of the wage, enabling companies to adjust labor costs to changing production and profit targets. Being from one to four minutes late on three occasions or taking sick leave are enough to forfeit one's bonus.[22] Women who refuse night work may be denied bonuses or dismissed.

Stress and high anxiety permeate the women's work lives, contributing to health problems. Most factories operate several shifts, requiring workers to rotate day and night shifts every week or two. These irregular schedules wreak havoc with sleep patterns and foster nervous ailments and stomach disorders. Lunch breaks may be barely long enough for a woman to stand in line at the canteen. Visits to the bathroom are treated as a privilege; in some cases workers must raise their hands for permission to use the toilet. Waits up to a half hour are common. When production deadlines draw near or there are rush orders, women may be forced to work overtime for as much as 48 hours at a stretch. Management often provides pep pills and amphetamine injections to keep the women awake and working; some of the women have become addicts.[23]

Sexual harassment is another hazard of factory work, especially for women who are out late at night working the graveyard shift. In the Bataan Export Processing Zone in the Philippines, sexual harassment is a common practice among male supervisors. "We call our company 'motel,'" says a worker at Mattel, "because we are often told to lay down or be laid off. It is hard to know what to do when that happens because we can't afford to lose our jobs."[24]

After the initial glamour has worn off the job, women may start to wonder what they've gotten themselves into. A variety of management control techniques are used to deactivate worker dissatisfaction and prevent women from organizing. The larger the company, the more sophisticated and subtle the methods.

At Fairchild Camera and Instrument in Hong Kong and South Korea, business school students from local universities try out the latest scientific management practices. To keep workers out of the General Electronics Union, which was involved in two strikes, one Fairchild manager created a "Joint Consultation Committee" of workers and managers to personalize worker problems and block collective action.[25] Company-sponsored recreational activities are designed to waylay demands for job improvements. A U.S. plant manager in Malaysia says, "We've developed recreation to a technique," with sewing classes, singing competitions and sports events.[26]

Multinationals pit women against each other not only as workers, but also as sex objects, superimposing Western notions of

Mattel Philippines, Inc., Bataan Export Processing Zone, The Philippines

femininity and consumerism upon local cultural stereotypes. Beauty contests are an integral part of factory life, with each company sending its own beauty queen to the yearly "Miss Free Trade Zone" contest. Bathing suit and "Guess-whose-legs-these-are" contests are also popular. On payday, vendors are often let into the factories to sell cosmetics (promoted in company-sponsored cosmetics classes), jewelry and other luxury items.

Naturally, women's entry into the workforce has dramatic effects in countries where their lives have always been centered around the family and home production. On the one hand, factory work does offer women some autonomy, earning power and freedom from parental control. In Malaysia, says Rachel Grossman, "They come for the money of course, but also for the freedom. They talk of freedom to go out late at night, to have a boyfriend, to wear blue jeans, high-heeled shoes and makeup...They revel in their escape from the watchful eyes of fathers and brothers."[27]

On the other hand, factory workers often pay a high price for that newly won freedom, limited though it may be. Because of their relative independence, Westernized dress and changed lifestyles, women may be rejected by their families and find it hard to reassimilate when they can no longer find employment on the assembly line. "Factory girls," especially those living away from their families in company dormitories or urban housing are thought to be "loose" sexually. The issue of women workers' morality is a burning one in many East Asian countries, debated by women's groups, politicians and community leaders.

Women who work in factories are often scorned by men as unsuitable marriage partners. Although pressure to marry is great, women have a harder time finding a mate after spending their prime marriageable years in the factory. By age 27 or 28, an unmarried woman is something of a misfit and if she has worked in a factory, the stigma is even greater. Competition among the workers for eligible husbands is intense. Social isolation, says Linda Gail Arrigo, is a growing problem among these young women. Caught between traditional roles and their new status as workers, the "Oriental girls" are at home nowhere.

"Hospitality Girls"

The growth of multinational enterprises in East Asia is directly tied to the rise of tourism and the "hospitality industry," a euphemism for organized prostitution, employing thousands of women. An advertisement for the Rosie Travel Company in Thailand reads:

Thailand is a world full of extremes and the possibilities are unlimited.

> Anything goes in this exotic country. Especially when it comes to girls.
> Still it appears to be a problem for visitors to Thailand to find the right
> places where they can indulge in unknown pleasures. Rosie has done
> something about this. For the first time in history you can book a trip to
> Thailand with erotic pleasures included in the price...[28]

For Noi, a 20-year-old Thai woman, prostitution provides a des-
perately-needed second income. "I get 25 *baht* per day" [then worth
less than $1.50] working in a battery factory, she explains. "But this is
not enough to cover my expenses. How could this be enough to pay
for my food, my bus ticket and other expenses? And I can tell you I
am thrifty. I have to find work at night so that I can send money to
my parents."[29] Many other prostitutes are former factory workers,
desperate for employment, or young women who came to the cities
looking for factory work they never found.

In the Philippines, tourism is part of the government's strategy
for development; it is the country's fourth largest source of foreign
exchange. Its success stems from its "hospitality industry" which
caters to male tourists, primarily from Japan. Officially, there are
about 100,000 "hostesses," representing those women who have
received government permits to work in licensed businesses, such as
bars and cafes. But an accurate figure must include streetwalkers,
call girls and brothel workers, none of whom are registered with the
government.

Travel agencies in Japan and the Philippines arrange package
tours to Manila that offer everything from accommodations to
shopping to escort-women who are selected during tours of night
clubs and cabarets. A man can buy a woman for the night for $60.
After the club owner and tour guides take their cut, she may receive
$6. Some of the best hotels in Manila, built for an IMF/World Bank
convention in 1976, now rely on prostitution to boost low occu-
pancy rates.[30]

Tourism is also a big industry in South Korea, with revenues of
$270 million a year. *Kiasaeng* (prostitutes) are responsible for this
success. Although the Law on Decadent Acts includes a strict
anti-prostitution code, *kiasaeng* are regularly issued ID cards by the
government to allow them into tourist areas to work. Travel
agencies in Japan advertise South Korea as a "male paradise"
offering tours that include *kiasaeng* parties, *kiasaeng* restaurants
and *kiasaeng* houses. A tourist can buy a South Korean woman for
$75-a-night with the expectation, encouraged by the industry, that
she will do anything to please him. This male paradise also caters to
multinational businessmen, U.S. military personnel and government officials. Multinational corporations and banks have invested
heavily in the hotels, agencies and transportation systems that
support *kiasaeng* tourism.[31]

3

SOUTH OF THE BORDER, DOWN MEXICO WAY

> Have your cake and eat it too...Live in the U.S. Pay your [Mexican] employees $6.64 a day.
>
> Advertisement in an El Paso business publication

For tourists, Mexico is the land of cheap vacations, spicy food and *sombreros*. For U.S. business, Mexico is the land of cheap labor. Southwestern agribusiness has long been dependent on that labor in the form of *mojados* (wetbacks) who slip across the border for work.

From 1942 to 1964 the Bracero Program regulated the flow of *braceros* (contracted migrant workers) into the United States. When the program was stopped, 200,000 farm workers were suddenly jobless. Unemployment reached 50 percent among the manual laborers in border cities like Mexicali and Ciudad Juarez. The Mexican government, anxious for a solution to the crisis, reacted enthusiastically when the Mexican secretary of industry and commerce was invited to visit new U.S. assembly plants in Hong Kong and Taiwan. U.S. industrialists proposed the creation of a free trade zone on the U.S.-Mexican border that would both fulfill U.S. manufacturers' need for cheap labor and create jobs for Mexico's unemployed.[32] Mexican officials assumed (wrongly, it turned out) that transfer of technology and skills would be part of the bargain. Thus was born the Border Industrialization Program (BIP) in 1965 with the *maquiladora* system of twin plants, one on either side of the border. Labor-intensive processes were to be located in Mexico. Pre-cut garments, electronic components

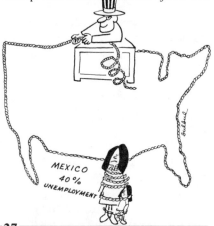

MEXICO
40%
UNEMPLOYMENT

Tikal de Mexico, Tijuana

and artificial flowers, among other things, would be sent from U.S.-based plants to the maquiladora for sewing, welding, gluing and assembly and shipped back to the U.S. for distribution.

Unprecedented financial incentives were granted to foreign companies by the Mexican government: factories could be 100 percent foreign-owned and managed; low taxes on profits and sales were offered, with some Mexican states giving full tax exemption; and land could be purchased or leased on favorable terms. Unofficially, corporations were given carte blanche to conduct business and labor affairs without government interference.

The Mexican government had considered BIP a temporary response to a crisis situation. But in 1972, BIP was expanded from the original 12.5 mile stretch of the border to include all of Mexico, opening up the entire country to a new form of colonization in which labor, not raw materials, was the main prize.[33]

Maquila Women

From the start, BIP was a lopsided arrangement, offering Mexico little in return for its concessions. Rather than alleviate massive unemployment among male workers in the border area, the program targeted a new source of cheap factory labor. Corporations aimed to draw unprecedented numbers of women into the industrial labor force just as they had done in East Asia. Arthur D. Little, a U.S. consulting firm that had designed several industrial parks under BIP, did a study in 1966 that outlined strategy for U.S.

business on the border: "The present industrial pool of about 25,000 can increase severalfold through greater use of female labor (only one-fifth of the labor pool is female at present), through the conversion to industrial work of low-income agricultural and commercial labor, and through the attraction of further immigration from central Mexico."[34]

By 1974, there were about 500 maquiladoras operating on the border, employing some 80,000 people, 85 percent of whom were women. The majority were between 16 and 25 years old and came to the border zone from small towns and cities. Entire families moved north in the hope that their daughters could find work. Mexican women were targeted for assembly jobs for the same reasons as their Asian sisters—they could be paid less than men because of their disadvantaged position in society and because their wages were considered only supplementary to male sources of family income. Maquiladora workers average 48 hours a week on the job for the minimum wage of 455 pesos a day—about 77 U.S. cents an hour. (With the recent devaluations of the Mexican peso, the real wages of Mexican workers have dropped sharply.)

As in East Asia, low wages aren't the only reason multinationals prefer women. Social and cultural stereotypes of docile and uncomplaining "girls" apply here as well. A primer for businesses setting up maquiladoras states that "from their earliest conditioning women show respect and obedience to authority,

Audio-Magnetics plant, Tijuana

COMO: SELF-HELP FOR
MEXICAN WOMEN

Local, grassroots projects are necessary building blocks in challenging multinational domination. In Ciudad Juarez, the Center for the Orientation of the Working Woman (COMO) is such a project. Since 1970 the Center has existed to serve the needs of working women, especially former maquiladora workers.

Through consciousness-raising and education, COMO helps women cope with the dislocations of border life and use their work experiences to help themselves and other women gain more control over their lives. Women are trained as social promoters, helping people to organize cooperative enterprises and teaching them accounting and managerial skills. For example, ten displaced maquiladora seamstresses formed a cloth manufacturing cooperative. COMO's vocational training prepares women to be social workers, teaching assistants, nurses aides, cooperative technicians and personnel management aides.

COMO's structure and activities have changed over the years, reflecting the constant input of the women who participate. As an organization that orients women to the social, political and economic realities of Mexican society and offers alternatives to factory work, COMO has gained international recognition as a prototype.

especially men. The women follow orders willingly, accept change and adjustments easily and are considerably less demanding..." According to an electronics plant manager in Ciudad Juarez men are much more difficult: "The man in Mexico is still the man. This kind of job is not doing much for his macho image. It's just a little quirk of a different culture. They'd rather run a factory."[35]

There are presently over 600 maquiladoras on the border, accounting for half of all the assembled products which enter the U.S. under lenient tariff codes designed to nurture offshore manufacturing. With companies streaming down to the border to exploit Mexico's growing economic difficulties—aggravated by the drop in oil export earnings—the future of the maquiladora looks rosy.

The picture is not so rosy, however, for the 135,000 women working the maquiladoras, nor the hundreds of thousands who will be drawn into the labor market in the coming years. The National Bank of Mexico predicts that the maquiladora workforce will reach half a million by 1990. Companies routinely violate federal labor laws on minimum wages and social security and frequently require women to sign temporary work contracts to prevent them from accruing seniority and the increased salaries that go with it. As in the Philippines, a medical certificate proving that a job applicant is not pregnant is often required, eliminating any expenses for maternity benefits.

Workers in electronics plants, which account for 60 percent of the maquiladoras, are regularly exposed to toxic chemicals. Because women's work is assumed to be a temporary hiatus from their usual domestic tasks, health and safety concerns are brushed aside. "We don't worry too much about these matters; these girls don't stay on the job long enough to get sick," claims a plant manager in Ciudad Juarez.[36] But in garment factories, which comprise 30 percent of all border industry, chronic back problems, asthma, conjunctivitis, bronchitis and brown-lung are common occupational diseases. With the intense pressure of assembly work, maquila women experience high levels of gastro-intestinal disorders, insomnia and menstrual irregularities. Bladder problems are common because women cannot use the toilets or drink water freely.

Almost two decades after the first maquiladora started operating, BIP is generally recognized as a failure in terms of the Mexican government's initial expectations. Male unemployment along the border has reached 67 percent; transfer of skills to the workforce and technology to Mexican industry has been minimal (learning to stitch 1,000 shirt cuffs per day may lead to a shirt sleeve, but not much else); and capital-intensive technology remains in the U.S. Adding insult to injury, up to 70 percent of maquiladora workers' wages are spent across the border in the United States and do not

Gary Massoni

contribute to the Mexican economy.[37] What began as a short-term remedy for Mexico's economic malaise, has only deepened dependency on the U.S. and generated new problems for the Mexican people.

"Las Mujeres Son Buenas Para El Metate y El Petate"
(Women are Good in the Kitchen and the Bedroom)

In a society that considers woman's "proper place" to be "in the kitchen and the bedroom," the employment of women in maquiladoras is disrupting the status quo. As a result of male under- and unemployment, women are often the main source of income for their families. In fact, an increasing number of Mexican women— between 20 and 30 percent of the female workforce—are heads of households. The trend is especially marked among garment workers, who tend to be older than other assembly workers and to have children.[38]

Maria Isela Torres, a maquiladora worker for ten years, believes factory work "has given us, women with few options, the opportunity for honest employment. For many it means not having to work as domestics in the U.S. or in disreputable places."[39] The Mexican government and the multinationals claim that factory work emancipates women by giving them earning power and independence. The governor of Chihuahua, a border state with many foreign-owned factories, asserts "the maquiladoras have

PRO

Here's why you should locate your next plant in Ciudad Juarez

★ Low cost, highly efficient labor with extremely low turnover and absenteeism rates.

★ Excellent labor relations atmosphere.

★ Greatest availability of skilled, semi-skilled, and unskilled personnel anywhere along the Mexican border.

★ Largest pool of technical, managerial, and administrative manpower resources along the border.

Duty free imports for machinery and raw Mexico, low duty rates on ducts when

Gary Massoni

turned out to work in favor of women's liberation, more than anything else."[40] In Ciudad Juarez—where there are over one hundred maquiladoras—banks, bars, clothing stores and discotheques now cater to the maquila woman.

But buying power is not social power. There is a growing backlash against maquila women, as men attempt to preserve their dominance over the family and society. Male resentment and hostility toward working women has led to the stigmatization of maquila women. They are seen as immoral and as destroying the family. A "bad reputation" goes along with the factory job. Anthropologist Patricia Fernandez Kelly, who worked in a garment maquiladora, reported that in northern Mexico the tabloids delight in playing up stories of scandal in the maquiladora: indiscriminate sex on the job, epidemics of venereal disease, fetuses found in factory rest rooms. As one woman told her, "I worry about this because there are those who treat you differently as soon as they know you have a job at a maquiladora. Maybe they think that if you have to work there's a chance you're a whore." Fernandez Kelly believes that stigmatization of working women serves to keep them in line. "You have to think of the kind of socialization that girls experience in a very Catholic society. The fear of having a 'reputation' is enough to make a lot of women bend over backward to be respectable and ladylike, which is just what management wants."

4

THE INTERNATIONAL TRAFFIC IN WOMEN

Third World governments are often willing partners in the exploitation of working women. The government treasuries gain little direct revenue from this kind of investment, because of all the financial incentives they offer. But host governments can count on economic and military assistance from the U.S. and other Western countries and receive loans from multinational banks and lending agencies. Government

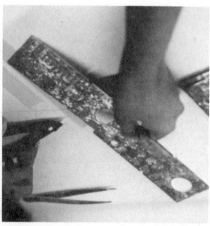

Linda Gail Arrigo

officials enrich themselves by specializing in cutting red tape for an "agent's fee" or an outright bribe, and Harvard- or Berkeley-educated technocrats assume a privileged niche as local managers.

In the competition for corporate investment, prospective host governments advertise women shamelessly. The Royal Thai embassy sends U.S. businesses a brochure guaranteeing that in Thailand, "the relationship between the employer and the employee is like that of a guardian and a ward. It is easy to win and maintain the loyalty of workers as long as they are treated with kindness and courtesy." The facing page offers a highly selective photo-study of Thai women: giggling shyly, bowing submissively and working cheerfully on an assembly line.

Many governments are willing to back up their advertising

with whatever amount of repression it takes to keep "their girls" as docile as they appear in the brochures. A feature of martial law in the Philippines, for example, is the New Labor Code, which President Marcos instituted to stifle increasing labor unrest. The code bans all strikes in "vital industries," including all industries in the export processing zones, and permits companies to suspend any worker "who poses a serious danger to the life or property of the employer"—a statute that is frequently interpreted to block all forms of labor activism.

Even the most moderate and orderly attempts to organize are likely to bring down heavy doses of police brutality.

• In **Guatemala**, in 1975, women workers in a U.S. factory, producing jeans and jackets, drew up a list of complaints that included insults by management, piecework wages that were less than the legal minimum, no overtime pay and "threats of death." The U.S. boss made a quick call to the local authorities to report that he was being harassed by "communists." When the women reported to work the next day they found the factory surrounded by heavily armed contingents of military police. The "communist" organizers were identified and fired.

• In the **Dominican Republic**, in 1978, workers who attempted to organize at the La Romana industrial zone were fired and then arrested by the local police. The zone has been described by U.S. unions as a "modern slave labor camp." Workers who do not meet

Linda Gail Arrigo

Ampex, Taiwan

Women and the Global Assembly Line Project

Bataan Export Processing Zone, The Philippines

their production quotas during regular shifts must put in unpaid overtime until they do meet them and women workers are often strip-searched at the end of the day. During the 1978 union-organizing attempt the government sent in national police armed with automatic weapons. Gulf & Western, the dominant multi-national in the country, augments local law enforcement with its own company-sponsored motorcycle club, which specializes in terrorizing suspected union sympathizers.

• In **Inchon, South Korea**, women at the Dong-Il Textile Company, a producer of fabrics and yarn for export to the U.S., had succeeded in gaining leadership in their union local in 1972. In 1978 the government-controlled, male-dominated Federation of Korean Trade Unions sent special "action squads" to destroy the women's union. Armed with steel bars and buckets of human excrement, the goons broke into the union office, smashed the office equipment and smeared the excrement over the women's bodies and in their ears, eyes and mouths.

Banking on Cheap Labor

Crudely put, the relationship between many Third World governments and multinational corporations is like that of a pimp and his customers. The governments advertise their women, sell

Women and the Global Assembly Line Project

El Salvador

them and keep them in line for the multinational "johns." But there are other parties to the growing international traffic in women: Western governments, the World Bank, the International Monetary Fund (IMF) and the United Nations Industrial Development Organization (UNIDO).

UNIDO has been a major promoter of export production and free trade zones since 1970, when it began providing assistance on different aspects of zone development. In 1976 it organized an international association of free trade zones whose express purpose was to open up Third World countries to the activities of multinational corporations.[41]

The World Bank, an international lending and development agency dominated by the U.S., is another architect of the global assembly line.* Although the Bank professes to be apolitical, the Ascher Memorandum, a secret World Bank report leaked to the press in late 1980, suggests otherwise: "The World Bank's imprimatur on the industrial program [in the Philippines] runs the risk of drawing criticism of the Bank as the servant of multinational

---

* The current president of the World Bank is A.W. Clausen, former president of the Bank of America. Clausen succeeded Robert McNamara who, before heading the World Bank, served as secretary of defense for Presidents Kennedy and Johnson.

"MASS HYSTERIA:"
JOB AILMENT, JOB ACTION

Outbreaks of "mass hysteria" have occurred along the global assembly line from Malaysia to the mid-western United States. In Malaysia, a woman may suddenly see a *hantu* or *jin*, a hideous mythological spirit, while peering through a microscope. She falls to the floor in convulsions, screaming with *masuk hantu*, spirit possession. Within minutes the hysteria spreads up and down the assembly line. Sometimes factories must be closed for a week or more while the evil spirits are exorcised.

Western managers have tried Valium and smelling salts. They have tried goat sacrifices and engaged the services of *bomohs*, traditional healers, to prevent hysteria from paralyzing production. But hysteria may be a traditionally-based reaction to ultra-modern exploitation. In Malaysia, where labor unions are outlawed, women have virtually no other outlets to protest working conditions. For instance, a shoe factory in Malacca had 40 incidents in two years. Not coincidentally, the factory had terrible working conditions: no medical benefits, no grievance procedures, a wage rate of $1.50 per day and a spy system which insured an atmosphere of intimidation.

Malaysian researchers who have studied the phenomenon note that outbreaks of "mass hysteria" are likely to be preceded by a speed-up or tightening of discipline in the factory. "Hysteria is an expression of hostility without physical violence," says Teoh Jin Inn, a Kuala Lumpur psychiatrist.

Thousands of miles away, in a shoe factory in the mid-

corporations and particularly of U.S. economic imperialism."[42] Bank loans to Third World countries are generally conditioned upon compliance with the Bank's own economic blueprint; this usually includes elimination of import tariffs that protect domestic industry but hamper multinationals, tax breaks for foreign investors and the creation of free trade zones. The Sri Lankan garment industry, for example, set up with a $20 million loan and advice from the World Bank, offers young women jobs at a global low of $5 for a six-day work week.

The World Bank's policies reflect little concern for the

western United States, women workers reacted much like their Malaysian sisters, with a few cultural variants. When a new batch of glue was opened one morning, four women grew faint and had to stop working. The next day several more workers had headaches, nausea, blurred vision, muscle soreness and chest pains. The management evacuated the plant under a pretext, but rumors of dangerous fumes spread through the crowd of employees waiting around the parking lot and 48 more workers were striken. Inspectors from the Occupational Safety and Health Administration examined the plant, but found no trace of toxins. Another plant had 20 similar incidents in 18 months.

Claudia Miller, an industrial hygienist, believes that many people are sensitive to minute quantities of chemicals, far below acceptable levels set by OSHA. Psychologist Michael Colligan, who has studied mass psychogenic illness, believes such incidents are a combination of both physical and psychological stresses. Conditions of poor ventilation, bad lighting and chemical fumes combine with the monotony and pressure of assembly line work, aggravating the workers' feelings of dissatisfaction and discomfort. A chemical odor or other physical hazard can touch off a contagious reaction.

"Mass hysteria" is a misleading term which demeans women workers and masks unhealthy, repressive working conditions. Whether it's a physical job-related ailment or a job action, or a combination of both, "hysteria" may be the healthiest response available.

Sources: Maria Patricia Fernandez Kelly, "Women's Industrial Employment, Migration and Health Status Along the U.S.-Mexican Border," working paper for the program in U.S.-Mexican Studies, University of California, San Diego, 1981.

repressive nature of many Third World governments it supports. In fact, rightwing, anti-labor governments are often favored by the Bank. The Philippines is a good case in point. For the three years preceding martial law, the World Bank provided the Philippine government with $320 million in aid. But after Marcos initiated his repressive policies in 1972, including a ban on strikes, and government control of unions, over $2.4 billion in Bank loans were poured into the country between 1973 and 1981. Bank officials expressed satisfaction that martial law gave Marcos "almost absolute power in the field of economic development" leading to "a significant

Haiti

Women and the Global Assembly Line Project

improvement in economic and financial management."[43]

Gloria Scott, head of the World Bank's Women and Development Program, defended the Bank's role in promoting factory work for Third World women. "Our job is to help eliminate poverty. It is not our responsibility if the multinationals come in and offer such low wages. It's the responsibility of the governments," she claims— as if low wages and poverty were unrelated. Actually, the Bank shares direct responsibility; in its 1979 *World Development Report*, it strongly urges wage restraint in poor countries.

The International Monetary Fund, companion institution to the World Bank, functions as the premier international credit agency. Cheryl Payer, an expert on the IMF and World Bank, explains that "all of the major sources of credit in the developed capitalist world, whether private lenders, governments, or multilateral institutions such as the World Bank group, will refuse to lend to a country which persists in defying IMF 'advice.' " The IMF's standard "stabilization" program includes control of wages; abolition of price controls and any subsidies for food and other necessities; increases in taxes; and the dismantling of any policies such as import and export controls that are seen as unfavorable to foreign investors. One result of IMF "stabilization" of Indonesia in the 1960s was the decimation of the domestic textile industry.[44]

Uncle Sam's Helping Hand

The most powerful promoter of exploitative conditions for Third World women workers is the U.S. government. The notorious South Korean textile industry was developed with $400 million in U.S. aid. Malaysia became a low-wage haven for the electronics industry with assistance from the U.S. Agency for International Development. Taiwan's status as a "showcase for the Free World" and a comfortable berth for multinational corporations is the result of three decades of U.S. economic and military support.

Non-governmental agencies work directly with AID and the State Department, or covertly with the CIA to cultivate support and derail opposition in Third World countries. For example, the AFL-CIO's Asian-American Free Labor Institute (AAFLI) ostensibly works to encourage "free" (read pro-capitalist) trade unions in Asia, but its actual mission is to discourage progressive, mass-based worker activity. AAFLI is very active in the Philippines and works with the Federation of Korean Trade Unions, which was responsible for the attack on the women's textile union described above. In Latin America, the American Institute for Free Labor Development (AIFLD) serves the same purpose, coopting or destroying genuine worker organizing attempts.[45]

The most blatant form of U.S. involvement, explains Lenny

Siegel, director of the Pacific Studies Center, is "our consistent record of military aid to Third World governments that are capitalist, politically repressive and are not striving for economic independence." Thailand has been ruled by a military junta since 1976. Singapore's dictator Lee Kuan Yew took power in 1959, repressing students, unionists, leftists and the media. Indonesia's bloody 1965 coup ushered in the regime of Suharto, who placed strict controls on labor organizing, including the banning of strikes. Malaysia has labor ordinances restricting unionization and the unions which do exist are weak and ineffective. The Marcos

ECONOMIC FREEDOM IN GUATEMALA

In 1982, CBS News presented an unusually candid report on Guatemala by correspondent Ed Rabel. It featured an interview with the former head of the U.S. Chamber of Commerce in Guatemala, Fred Sherwood, who took no pains to hide his approval of state terrorism in the service of business interests (including some 200 U.S. corporations). Sherwood himself owns a rubber plantation, a cement factory and a textile mill where he pays his workers about $4.50 a day.

RABEL: ...The whole country of Guatemala was once virtually a branch office of the United Fruit Company. In the 1950s, it held two-thirds of the usable farmland and monopolized the nation's railroads in its multimillion-dollar banana empire. When a democratically elected president named Jacobo Arbenz tried to institute a land reform program in 1954 so poor farmers could have land of their own, United Fruit lobbied the Eisenhower Administration to intervene. The CIA stepped in and overthrew the Guatemalan leader...[Sherwood says] it's an ideal place to invest...because profits are high, costs are low.

SHERWOOD: We have a large labor market and the workers are very good. You teach them and they—they don't mind doing the same thing day after day, the routine, like American workers like a variation. But here, the people do the same thing day after day, and they're very good.

RABEL: Is the government pretty cooperative?

SHERWOOD: Oh, yes. They're very cooperative. We don't have restrictions as to environmental things and there's just no restrictions or rules at all, so that makes it nice.

dictatorship in the Philippines has been cited by Amnesty International for its consistent record of human rights violations and repression. In 1977, combined military aid from the U.S. to those five countries was nearly half a billion dollars.[46]

Governments that aren't properly supportive of multinational corporate interests may be "destabilized" by U.S.-backed interventions aimed at installing ones which are. In 1954 in Guatemala and in 1973 in Chile, democratically elected, reform-minded presidents were ousted from office by U.S.-backed military coups. A picture of conditions in Guatemala is given in the box below.

RABEL: Are the people here oppressed in any way?

SHERWOOD: Really, I don't think so. I know of no individual, I know of no one—I have lived here for 36 years, I've been in farming, in industry, in commerce—and I don't know of anybody being impressed [sic]. No one forces them to do anything. And I think this is just something that some reporters have thought up.

RABEL: Most Guatemalans see a different country than Fred Sherwood does. Human rights organizations have repeatedly accused Guatemalan governments of running deliberate programs of political murder to maintain a grip on power...priests, nuns, labor leaders, teachers, students—anyone who threatened the established order. Politicians have always been high on the hit list...a [Christian Democrat] politician here in this country told me...that more than 120 of his party's leaders had been assassinated in about an 18-month period...

SHERWOOD: Well, first place, I'd very much question it, because I don't think there's been a hundred and twenty people of all types assassinated here in the—in the last year. I mean, I'm not counting the peasants or the—I mean men of that category. No, I think that's probably exaggerated to a great extent. There were a couple of politicians assassinated a couple years ago, but believe me, they were way out in left field and well, these people are, I think, our enemies. They're—they're against our—our way of life. And maybe assassination is not the right word for it, but I don't think they should be—continue allowed to run free to try to destroy our form of government, our way of life in other words.

Source: CBS Reports, "Guatemala," with CBS News correspondent Ed Rabel, broadcast September 1, 1982.

At the Department of State, a spokesman insisted that if multinationals provide poor working conditions—which he questioned—this was not their fault: "There are just different standards in different countries." He insisted that "corporations today are generally more socially responsible than even ten years ago...We can expect them to treat their employees in the best way they can." But, he conceded in response to a barrage of unpleasant examples, "Of course you're going to have problems wherever you have human beings doing things." At the Women's Division of AID, staffer Emmy Simmons was aware of the criticisms of multinationals in the Third World, but cautioned, "We can get hung up on the idea that it's exploitation without really looking at the alternatives for women."

Third World Women Organize

For many young Third World women there is no immediate alternative to the assembly line. But that doesn't mean conditions can't be changed. In the face of government repression and corporate threats to "run away" to more hospitable sites, more and more women are organizing to fight for better wages and working conditions. The following sketches illustrate some of the many struggles which have taken place in the last decade:

• **Nuevo Laredo, Mexico, 1973:** Two thousand workers at Transitron Electronics walked out in solidarity with a small number of workers who had been fired unjustly. Two days later, 8,000 striking workers met and elected a more militant union leadership.

• **Mexicali, Mexico, 1974:** Three thousand workers locked out by Mextel, a Mattel subsidiary, set up a 24-hour guard to prevent the company from moving in search of cheaper labor. The company did move away, but only after two months of confrontations.

• **Taiwan, 1975:** Five thousand workers at General Instruments (the largest foreign employer) went on strike over a cut in bonus pay. Two thousand workers mobbed the personnel office. When the American vice-president threatened to take the company elsewhere, the Taiwan government invoked martial law powers. Union leaders responsible for the strike capitulated when faced with the threat of capital punishment.

• **Bangkok, Thailand, 1976:** Seventy young women locked out their Japanese bosses and took control of their garment factory. They continued to produce jeans and floppy hats for export, paying themselves 150 percent more than their bosses had.

• **Seoul, South Korea, 1977:** Women at Tae Hyup, an exclusive contractor for Mattel, staged a walk-out to protest low wages and poor working conditions. Though the police broke up the strike and no pay increases were won, church activists in the

El Salvador

Women and the Global Assembly Line Project

U.S. formulated a stockholder's resolution for Mattel to issue a code of labor standards for their overseas factories.

• **South Korea, 1979:** Two hundred young women employees of the YH textile and wig factory staged a peaceful vigil and fast to protest the company's threatened closing of the plant. On August 11, the fifth day of the vigil, more than 1,000 riot police armed with clubs and steel shields broke into the building where the women were staying and forcibly dragged them out. Twenty-one year old Kim Kyong Suk was killed during the melee. It was her death that touched off the widespread rioting throughout the country that many believe led to the overthrow of the dictator Park Chung Hee.

• **Ciudad Juarez, Mexico, 1980:** One thousand women workers occupied an American Hospital Supply Corporation factory after one hundred and eighty thugs entered the factory and beat up the women leaders. The women, mostly in their teens and early twenties, were demanding better working conditions, paid vacations and recognition of the union of their choice.

• **Bataan Export Processing Zone, Philippines, 1981:** Three thousand members of the Mattel Philippines workers union went out on strike to protest Mattel's violation of a starting wage agreement. The fifth strike in a year and a half, it was also the largest. Workers, the majority of them women, were expelled from the zone by force. In spite of the expulsion, back-to-work orders

Texas Instruments, Taiwan

Linda Gail Arrigo

Meat canning factory, Thailand

from the Ministry of Labor and threats of firing from Mattel, the workers continued their strike.

• **Zacatecas, Mexico, 1981:** Women at the U.S.-owned Crescent-Force garment plant waged a series of struggles over wages and union representation. Despite company dismissals of leadership and threats of further layoffs, the women continued to agitate for salary increases and reinstatement of those fired for union activities, winning small victories with the support of other Mexican unions and the townspeople of Zacatecas.

• **Bataan Export Processing Zone, Philippines, 1982:** Ten thousand workers went on strike in solidarity with two hundred employees at a Mitsubishi synthetics factory who had staged a walk-out after management increased the number of looms each worker operated from four to six. Workers were earning between $2.20 and $3.70 a day. When the zone police began brutalizing and arresting workers and protecting scabs, news of the clash spread quickly throughout the zone. By the third day of the strike, workers had halted production in 23 factories, forcing the government to meet with union representatives. Result: work loads were reduced and charges against jailed strikers were dropped. Less than two months later, Marcos shelved plans for six new zones and industrial parks.[47]

5

MADE IN THE USA

Not every manufacturer has the resources to run away to the cheap labor reservoirs of the Third World—nor do they need to. The same competition for profits that drives U.S. corporations abroad leads to substandard wages and labor abuses at home in the states. In the garment industry, sweatshops are proliferating at a rate unparalleled since the 19th century, when European immigrants  worked 12- to 16-hour days for pennies. The U.S. electronics industry, especially manufacturers of semiconductors, have scattered their assembly operations throughout the country in search of the cheapest labor and greatest tax breaks. While wages are relatively higher and conditions slightly better, working women in the U.S. (and other Western countries) are being shunted into jobs that threaten their health and economic well-being. The global assembly line begins and ends in our own backyard.

Twentieth Century Sweatshops

In Los Angeles, New York, Boston—anywhere the garment industry has taken root—unlicensed, substandard garment shops are springing up by the hundreds. Exact numbers are hard to come by since they operate illegally, on the fringes of the economy, to avoid unemployment insurance, minimum wage rates, child labor laws and overtime pay regulations. An organizer in Los Angeles reports that "people are working 16 and 18 hours a day. Or they work seven days a week without overtime. One woman I talked to this year put in a 60-hour-week and made $50."

Garment sweatshops come and go frequently in the melee of

Homeworking on the Lower East Side of Manhattan, 1890: The family of an immigrant tailor brings him the garments he will sew together at the rate of perhaps fifty cents for sixteen hours' work.

W. A. Rogers, Harper's Weekly, 1890

intense competition. Anyone with a few thousand dollars can start a shop with a dozen sewing machines, a neighborhood workforce and a low-rent building. The owners (or contractors) vie for orders from the jobbers, the middlemen to whom the large clothing manufacturers farm out bundles of pre-cut fabric for stitching. Neither the contractors nor the women they hire share in the huge profits collected by the jobbers and the big manufacturers. One contractor in New York's South Bronx says, "Do [the jobbers] pay enough? You've got to be kidding. They give you the cut material. They say the price they'll pay. So what can I do? I pay the girls $1.25 a dress. All I get is $2.60 and I've got to run the shop, rent machines, pay for electricity."

The "girls" clearly make out the worst in the sweatshop scenario. Ninety percent of the sweatshop workers in this country are female and the majority of these are immigrants from the Caribbean, Central America and Asia. Third World women are industry's best labor bargain, wherever they are found.

Sweatshop workers are women with few options. Many are heads of households who need a steady income to support their families. They are mothers without daycare who are often able to bring their children to the shop. Some are women who can't find better-paying jobs, but can't subsist on welfare alone, so they are forced to rely on the sweatshops for unreported income. Still others enter sweatshops to supplement inadequate old-age pensions.

A large portion of all sweatshop workers are undocumented; that is, they have entered the U.S. through extra-legal channels and don't possess the proper immigration papers. These women are particularly vulnerable to exploitation because they cannot.work in licensed businesses where they would have to show identification and Social Security numbers. Contractors frequently use the threat of deportation to maintain abusive work conditions and keep the women away from unions. One classic example, recounted in literature from the International Ladies Garment Workers Union (ILGWU) concerns a group of women who worked in a shop in Queens, New York. For many weeks, they worked from 7 a.m. to 11 p.m. with the promise of $15-per-day in wages. When their employer finally paid them, the checks bounced. The women went to the ILGWU for help, but when the union tried to intercede, the employer replied that he would pay them if they showed their "green cards," the required document for legal immigrants. This thinly veiled threat of deportation worked; the women never received their earnings.

Jobs in the garment sweatshops are easy to get and require little or no experience. Walk down 149th Street in the South Bronx in New York and you'll see one sign after another: "Se Necesita Operadoras," sewing machine operators wanted. Many also carry the promise of "Buena Paga," good pay. Damak Sportswear is a typical neighborhood garment operation. There, thirteen Puerto Rican women bend over Singer sewing machines in a poorly lit room that lacks fire alarms and a sprinkler system. Located on the third floor of an old tenement building, with wooden stairs and floor, the shop is a potential fire trap. But that is par for the course, according to Louis Berthold of the South Bronx Working Center, an ILGWU community outreach program. "One building on 161st Street had over forty health and fire violations and housed four shops. It wouldn't surprise me if there was another Triangle fire," he said, "the conditions are heading that way." (In 1911, 146 women working at the Triangle Shirtwaist factory in New York City died when a fire swept through the building. Doors and exits were

Susan E. Dorfman

Susan E. Dorfman

Garment workers, Massachusetts

blocked, trapping the women inside. Many leapt to their deaths from windows eight stories up.)

Exploitation of women workers isn't contained within the sweatshops. Homework is another labor abuse that is flourishing in the current economic climate. For jobbers, homework is a way to cut labor costs even further. Jobbers give women bundles of cut fabric to sew at home, pay less than shop wages and make the workers assume overhead costs such as purchase and repair of sewing machines, electricity and rent. Many homeworkers must enlist the help of their children to meet deadlines. As in the sweatshops, meeting the production quota is only part of the problem; collecting the promised wages is the other. A Haitian immigrant in Miami recounted her experience to the ILGWU: "I worked all the time, day and night, seven days a week. But my boss was no good. Once he gave me a bundle with 1,000 pieces in it. When I brought it back, he said it had had 2,000 pieces. He wouldn't pay me until I worked off the missing pieces."

Homeworking is so widespread and popular with contractors that even Nancy Reagan's high-fashion dresses may be "home-made." Her favorite designer, Adolpho, farms out his garment work to Ruth Fashions located in Queens. Ruth Fashions in turn farms it out to homeworkers. In 1982 the New York State Attorney General cited the company as a chronic violator of laws prohibiting homework.[48]

Often those who suffer most from homeworking and the sweat-shop system—undocumented women workers—are blamed for their very existence. But immigrants did not bring the miserable conditions with them in their luggage. A study of undocumented workers by the North American Congress on Latin America shows that labor abuse is not restricted to the undocumented, but rather, "these are the conditions of labor which now prevail in the sectors of industry where new immigrant workers, legal or not, come to dwell."[49]

Federal and state officials have done little to curb the growth of these industrial subcultures. And unions have so far had little effect organizing sweatshop workers. The ILGWU has begun only recently to confront the problem; it now campaigns for amnesty for undocumented immigrants, many of whom are garment workers the union would like to organize. Fear of losing their jobs, language barriers and the shadowy nature of the garment shops make organizing difficult. But occasionally women buck the odds to improve their working conditions. In 1975, 125 Chinese women at the Jung Sai garment shop in San Francisco conducted the longest strike in Chinese-American history to win an ILGWU contract. In 1977, 250 workers struck the W and W knitting mill in Brooklyn for six months. Seventy-five of the women were undocumented and risked deportation to march on the picket lines.[50]

Silicon Valley

Women mean cheap labor for the electronics industry, here or abroad. In Silicon Valley, near San Jose, California, 75 percent of

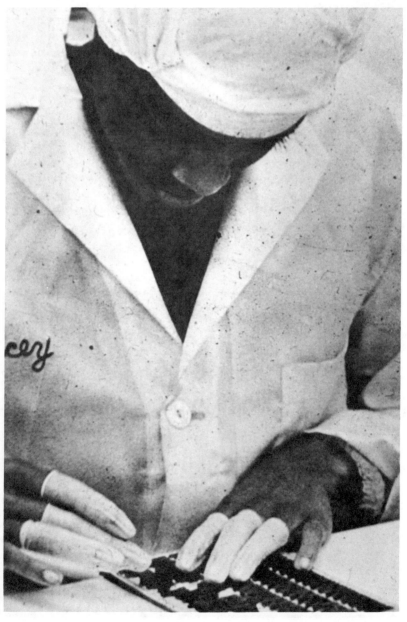

Leah Margulies and Holly Sklar, "Women and Global Corporations" slide show

the assembly line workers are women. The pattern is repeated along
Route 128, outside Boston, and in North Carolina, an anti-union,
"right to work" state now favored by the electronics industry. As in
the U.S. garment industry, immigrant women comprise a significant chunk of those workers: 40 percent. On the west coast,
Filipinas, Thais, Samoans, Mexicans and Vietnamese have made
the electronics assembly line a microcosm of the global production
process. Management exploits their lack of familiarity with English
and U.S. labor law. Often, companies divide the assembly line
according to race and nationality—one line may be all Vietnamese
while another is all Mexican—to encourage competition and
discourage cross-nationality alliances.

   Among the non-immigrant workers, many are married wom-
en, assuming paid employment after years of being homemakers.
Wages for semiconductor assembly in the U.S., while vastly
superior to those overseas, are among the lowest in all of U.S.
industry, averaging $6-an-hour after two or three years on the job.
Since there is little upward mobility for women, especially Third
World women, only a few ever attain the $6.50 to $9 an hour rate for
technical jobs. Only 19 percent of all technicians and less than 9
percent of managers are women.[51]

*'Before we demand that Congress protect our industry against cheap
foreign imports manufactured at slave labor wages, I'd like to remind
you, sir, that we own 67% of those foreign factories!'*

AFSC Women's Newsletter

The illness rate in the electronics industry is one of the highest. Women are regularly exposed to solvents which may cause menstrual and fertility problems, liver and kidney damage, cancer, and chemical hypersensitization, a condition which can leave them permanently allergic to a wide range of items from gasoline to hairspray. The federal Occupational Safety and Health Administration (OSHA), which is charged with enforcing safe and healthful working conditions, does not even have standards for many of the substances used in electronics plants.

Job security is next to nil. Michael Eisenscher, an organizer in Silicon Valley for the United Electrical, Radio and Machine Workers of America (UE), predicts decreasing job opportunities for women in the industry: "Everyone thinks of high technology as the future source of job growth, opportunities and innovation. But we've seen a contraction in jobs to the point where no one in the industry is hiring now. The economy is partly responsible, but another factor is that new technology demands automation." General Electric, which owns the semiconductor manufacturer,

Intersel, is aiming to replace 50 percent of its line workers with robots by the end of the 1980s. Eisenscher describes how companies get rid of workers while avoiding outright layoffs and unemployment compensation: women are assigned to different jobs or lines without retraining and then fired for low job performance.

There are no unionized semiconductor plants in the United States. Companies participate in seminars sponsored by the American Electronics Association to learn the latest anti-union techniques. Beer and pizza parties, awards and raffles for trips to Hawaii are used to convince people they don't need unions. Some of the techniques are much more blatant. When the president of National Semiconductor announced his decision to freeze wages, he had his speech videotaped with a live audience of managers and supervisors cheering in the background. The videotape was played 24 hours a day for three days in the cafeteria to convince workers of the necessity to "tighten their belts."

In February 1983, Atari, the videogame / home computer giant whose name has become a synonym for high technology, announced its plans to move most of its Silicon Valley production to Hong Kong and Taiwan (where electronics workers earn, respectively, $1.20 and 90 cents an hour in wages and benefits). Atari already has assembly plants in Singapore, Puerto Rico and Ireland. The Glaziers and Glassworkers Union sees this as another example of a company running away to avoid unionization and has filed a complaint with the National Labor Relations Board. According to union organizer Edward Jones, when the Glaziers drive began in 1982 the signed union cards "came flooding in." Atari responded with an anti-union petition, a slew of company-sponsored parties and problem-airing "communications meetings" before it took the ultimate step—the plant shutdown.[52]

UE is another union that has made a commitment to tackling the semiconductor industry, and has been in Silicon Valley for ten years, building awareness and support for organizing campaigns. At present, it is involved in an industrywide organizing drive, focusing on National Semiconductor and Signetics, a subsidiary of North American Philips Corporation. "When workers are prepared to take on the boss, language is no problem," says Eisenscher. "We minimize the barriers by issuing materials in two or three different languages, and have an active program of connecting with immigrant communities among Filipinos, Koreans, Vietnamese, as well as among older groups, like Latinos and Chinese." UE has also initiated links with the KMU, the major opposition labor federation in the Philippines. "Country-hopping won't resolve the world economic crisis for multinationals," says Eisenscher. "The system is simply not working." ●

6

THE ANSWER IS GLOBAL

Women all over the world are becoming a giant reserve army of labor at the disposal of globe-trotting multinationals. No woman can feel job security on the assembly line as long as the profit motive guides multinational activities. Runaways are now occurring *within* the Third World. Sri Lanka, which recently opened an export processing zone, has become a haven for companies fleeing the labor militancy in South Korea and the Philippines.

Charito Planas, former director of the Philippine Chamber of Commerce and now a Marcos opponent living in exile, says many women do not realize they're being exploited. "Because we've been dominated by foreigners, women employed in foreign corporations feel superior to those in local factories owned by Filipino businessmen...But there are some women who are aware of their situation and are organizing and involved in the struggle for better working conditions. Their numbers are growing despite government arrests. It's just a matter of time," she believes. "There's no stopping the pendulum of change."

Some corporate strategists are now suggesting that offshore factories are no longer viable. An editor of *Semiconductor International* argues that "if political turmoil begins to haunt the world, especially in those areas where U.S. companies have their assembly operations, it would be a disaster for the U.S. semiconductor industry...With the new, more vigorous U.S. defense posture, political polarization and turmoil are bound to occur. We can expect that some countries which now openly welcome the semiconductor industry will make greater demands on companies..."[53] The solution? Automated facilities in the United States to assure cheap labor *and* stability.

Automation without worker control and full employment is a threat to working people. In the electronics industry, women are assembling the very components which may be used to make their jobs and those of other workers obsolete. Faced with sexual and racial discrimination, women will be further hurt as remaining technical and managerial jobs go mainly to white men.

With continued economic crisis, when even low-paid jobs are hard to come by, it is especially easy for companies to play off their employees against each other. As sociologist Cynthia Enloe says, "We're all being fed the line that we are each other's competitors." Women in a Tennessee garment factory are threatened with competition from Mexican workers while women in the Philippines are threatened with competition from Sri Lanka. It's a competition in which all workers are losers; wages are driven down everywhere, and health and safety conditions deteriorate, but job security is never achieved. As garment worker Min Chong Suk asserts, "The people who are called economic scholars use 'international competition' when they talk. But we know they mean a way to squeeze workers."

Diego Rivera, The Militant/LNS

"Bound Together With One String"

Rachel Grossman argues, "Protectionism and nationalist attitudes that view Third World imports and workers as competition are lagging behind the times. The international nature of production has been an economic reality for some time now. Multinationals don't deal in terms of individual countries, but on a global scale." Any strategy to futher women's control over their worklives must take into account that new economic reality. Saralee Hamilton, coordinator of the AFSC Nationwide Women's Program says: "The multinational corporations have deliberately targeted women for exploitation. If feminism is going to mean anything to women all over the world, it's going to have to find new ways to resist corporate power internationally."

One way to resist that power is to use organized pressure in specific cases of corporate abuse. The boycott of Nestle products to protest their infant formula promotion in Third World countries is a good example of a successful consumer action. But a general boycott of consumer goods from Third World countries is unrealistic, and may hurt working people more than anything else.

Another important strategy is to foster an information exchange between Third World activists and their counterparts in the industrialized countries. Information on hazardous substances at the workplace or on corporate structures and strategies is often easier to obtain in the "home" countries of the multinationals where there are more resources at hand. Sharing the knowledge that will empower women workers in their struggle is a priority of solidarity work.

The most difficult, yet most important task in confronting multinational domination, is to create direct links between women workers around the world. International travel is expensive and few women have the money for long-distance phone calls or even postage. But some links are being made, such as UE's developing relationship with KMU of the Philippines. The Nationwide Women's Program organized a conference in 1978 on women and global corporations which brought together women from the Third World and the U.S. to share information and ideas. Out of that conference came the Women and Global Corporations project which encourages networking of working women in the Third World with women in the Western countries to provide support for their common struggles.

It may take years before international links are extensive and powerful enough to challenge successfully multinational corporations and the governments which support them, but women's lives grow closer all the time. "We all have the same hard life," wrote Min Chong Suk. "We are bound together with one string."   ●

FOOTNOTES

1. George Ball, "Cosmocorp: The Importance of Being Stateless," *Columbia Journal of World Business,* November/December 1967, p. 26.

2. Y.S. Chang, "The Transfer of Technology: Economics of Offshore Assembly: The Case of the Semiconductor Industry," United Nations Institute for Technology and Research (UNITAR), 1971.

3. Mary Alison Hancock, "The International Electronics Industry," working paper from the Culture Learning Institute, East-West Center, Honolulu, 1980, p. 14.

4. Tsuchaya Takeo, "What is the Free Trade Zone?" *AMPO: Japan-Asia Quarterly Review,* 1977, p. 1.

5. *Wall Street Journal,* December 9, 1980.

6. Philip Wheaton and Jeb Mays, *Puerto Rico: A People Challenging Colonialism,* (Washington, D.C.: Ecumenical Program for Inter-American Communication and Action [EPICA], 1976), pp. 23-24.

7. Michael Flannery, "America's Sweatshops in the Sun," *AFL-CIO American Federationist,* May 1978, p. 16.

8. Becky Cantwell, Don Luce and Leonard Weinglass, *Made in Taiwan* (New York: Asia Center, 1978) p. 14.

9. Amrita Chhachhi, "The Experiences of Retrenchment: Women Textile Workers in India," paper presented at textile workers conference of the Transnational Institute, Amsterdam, October 1981, p. 7.

10. From a slide show on women in the Philippines by the Philippine Solidarity Network, San Francisco, California.

11. "Our Fussy Factory Workers," *New Straits Times* (Singapore), June 18, 1978.

12. Richard L. Meier, "Multinationals as Agents of Social Development," *Bulletin of the Atomic Scientists,* November 1977, p. 32.

13. Heleieth I. B. Saffioti, "The Impact of Industrialization on the Structure of Female Employment," paper presented at textile workers conference of the Transnational Institute, Amsterdam, October 1981.

14. Linda Gail Arrigo, "The Industrial Workforce of Young Women in Taiwan," *Bulletin of Concerned Asian Scholars,* April-June 1980, p. 34.

15. "Export Processing Zones in Developing Countries," *UNIDO Working Papers on Structural Changes: 19* (Global and Conceptual Studies Section, International Center for Industrial Studies, United Nations Industrial Development Organization, August 18, 1980), p. 12.

16. *Ibid.,* p. 27.

17. Rachel Grossman, "Changing Role of Southeast Asian Women: The Global Assembly Line and the Social Manipulation of Women on the Job,"*Southeast Asia Chronicle, January-February 1979, p. 10.

18. Linda Y.C. Lim, "Women in the Redeployment of Manufacturing Industry to Developing Countries," *UNIDO Working Papers on Structural Changes: 18* (1980) p. 28.

19. *Global Electronics Information Newsletter* (Pacific Studies Center, Mountain View, California), February 1982.

20. Lim, "Women in the Redeployment of Manufacturing," p. 25.

21. Grossman, "Changing Role of Southeast Asian Women," p. 12.

22. Arrigo, "The Industrial Workforce of Young Women in Taiwan," pp. 32-33.

23. "Women Workers in Asia," *ISIS International Bulletin,* No. 10 (Rome and Geneva, Winter 1978/79), p. 12.

24. Philippine Solidarity Network slideshow.

25. Christina Tse, "The Invisible Control: Management Control of Workers in a U.S. Electronics Company," Center for the Progress of Peoples, Hong Kong, 1981, p. 16.

26. Grossman, "Changing Role of Southeast Asian Women," p. 4.

27. *Ibid.,* p. 13.

28. Illse Lenze, "Tourism Prostitution in Asia," *ISIS International Bulletin,* No. 13 (1979), p. 7.

29. Onze Wereld, "Sex Tourism to Thailand," *Ibid.,* p. 9.

30. A. Lin Neuman, "Hospitality Girls in the Philippines," *Southeast Asia Chronicle,* January-February 1979, p. 18.

31. Takahashi Kikue, 'Kiasaeng Tourism," *ISIS International Bulletin*, No. 13 (1979), p. 23.

32. Mario Arriola Woog, *El Programa Mexicana de Maquiladoras: una respuesta a las necesidades de la industria norteamericana* (Guadalajara: Universidad de Guadalajara, 1980), p. 50.

33. Maria Patricia Fernandez Kelly, "Women's Industrial Employment, Migration and Health Status Along the U.S.-Mexican Border," working paper for the Program in U.S.-Mexican Studies, University of California, San Diego, 1981, p.5.

34. "Hit and Run: U.S. Runaway Shops on the Mexican Border," *North American Congress on Latin America (NACLA): Latin America and Empire Report,* July-August 1975, p. 11.

35. *Cleveland Plain Dealer,* June 2, 1981.

36. Maria Patricia Fernandez Kelly, "Maquiladoras and Women in Ciudad Juarez: The Paradoxes of Industrialization under Global Capitalism," unpublished paper, Center for Latin American Studies, Stanford University, Palo Alto, California, no date given, p. 15.

37. Woog, *El Programa Mexicano de Maquiladoras,* p. 103.

38. Kelly, "Women's Industrial Employment," p. 10.

39. *Uno Mas Uno* (Mexico City), April 14, 1982.

40. Woog, *El Programa Mexicano de Maquiladoras,* p. 88.

41. Takeo, "What is the Free Trade Zone?" p. 4.

42. "The World Bank," *Southeast Asia Chronicle*, December 1981.

43. *Ibid.*

44. Cheryl Payer, *The Debt Trap* (New York: Monthly Review Press, 1974).

45. Lenny Siegel, "Orchestrating Dependency,"*Southeast Asia Chronicle,* January-February 1979, p. 26.

46. *Ibid.*

47. Henry Holland and Mimi Brady, "The Rise and Fall of EPZ's," *Economic and Political Weekly,* October 9, 1982, p. 1646.

48. *Mother Jones,* July 1982, p. 5.

49. Julia Preston, "Undocumented: Immigrant Workers in New York City," *NACLA Report on the Americas,* November-December 1979, p. 18.

50. *Ibid.* p. 42.

51. Marcie Axelrad, "Profile of the Electronics Industry Workforce in the Santa Clara Valley: A Preliminary Report from the Project on Health and Safety in Electronics (PHASE)," Santa Clara Center for Occupational Safety and Health, July 1979, p. 23.

52. Kathleen Sullivan, "Shutdown Sends PacMan to Asia," *In These Times*, March 23-29, 1983.

53. Donald J. Levinthal, "Automate, But Bring it Back Onshore," *Semiconductor International,* April 1981, p. 6.

SELECTED READINGS

Books, Articles and Pamphlets

Arrigo, Linda Gail. "The Industrial Work Force of Young Women in Taiwan." *Bulletin of Concerned Asian Scholars* 12:2 (April-June 1980).

Badillo-Vega, Americo: Dewind, Josh; Preston, Julia. "Undocumented: Immigrant Workers in New York City." *NACLA (North American Congress On Latin America) Report on the Americas.* November-December 1979.

Baird, Peter. "Hit and Run: Runaway Shops on the Mexican Border." *NACLA Report on the Americas* 9:5 (1975).

"Changing Role of Southeast Asian Women: The Global Assembly Line and the Social Manipulation of Women on the Job." *Southeast Asia Chronicle.* No. 66 and *Pacific Research* 9:5-6.

Chomsky, Noam and Herman, Edward. *The Political Economy of Human Rights.* Vol. 1. Boston: South End Press, 1979.

D'Onofrio-Flores, Pamela M. and Pfafflin, Sheila M., eds. *Scientific-Technological Change and the Role of Women in Development.* Boulder, Colorado: Westview Press/United Nations Institute for Training and Research, 1982.

Elson, Diane and Pearson, Ruth. "Nimble Fingers Make Cheap Workers: An Analysis of

Women's Employment in Third World Export Manufacturing." *Feminist Review.* Spring 1981.

Flynn, Patricia; Santana, Aracelly; Shapiro, Helen. "Latin American Women." *NACLA Report on the Americas.* October 1980.

"Free Trade Zones and Industrialization of Asia." *AMPO: Japan-Asia Quarterly Review.* Tokyo. 1977.

Kelly, Maria Patricia Fernandez. "The Maquila Women." in *Anthropology for the Eighties.* Johnetta Cole, ed. New York: The Free Press. 1982.

Lim, Linda Y.C. "Women in the Redeployment of Manufacturing Industry to Developing Countries." *United Nations Industrial Development Organization (UNIDO) Working Papers on Structural Changes.* No. 18 (July 1980).

_____. "Women Workers in Multinational Corporations: The Case of the Electronics Industry in Malaysia and Singapore." *Michigan Occasional Papers.* No. IX. Ann Arbor, Michigan: University of Michigan Women's Studies Program, 1978.

Magdoff, Harry. *Imperialism: From the Colonial Age to the Present.* New York: Monthly Review Press, 1978.

Nash, June. *Women and Men in the International Division of Labor.* Albany, New York: State University of New York, Albany, Press., 1983.

Payer, Cheryl. *The Debt Trap: The International Monetary Fund and the Third World.* New York: Monthly Review Press, 1974.

_____. *The World Bank: A Critical Analysis.* New York: Monthly Review Press, 1983.

Siegel, Lenny. "Delicate Bonds: The Global Semiconductor Industry." *Pacific Research* 11:1 (1980).

Sklar, Holly, ed. *Trilateralism: The Trilateral Commission and Elite Planning for World Management.* Boston: South End Press, 1980.

Stallard, Karin; Ehrenreich, Barbara; Sklar, Holly. *Poverty in the American Dream: Women and Children First.* New York/Boston: Institute for New Communications/South End Press, 1983.

Volk, Steve and Wishner, Amy. "Electronics: The Global Industry." *NACLA Report on the Americas* 11:4 (1977).

"Women and National Development." *Signs: Journal of Women in Culture and Society* 3:1 (Fall 1977).

Woog, Mario Arriola. *El Programa Mexicano de Maquiladoras: Una Respuesta a Las Necesidades de La Industria. Norteamericana.* Universidad de Guadalajara, Mexico, 1980.

RESOURCE ORGANIZATIONS

United States

American Friends Service Committee
Nationwide Women's Program/Women and Global Corporations Network
1501 Cherry Street
Philadelphia, Pennsylvania 19102

Center on Transnational Corporations
Room BR-1005
United Nations
New York, New York 10017

Data Center
Corporate Profiles Project
464 19th Street
Oakland, California 94612

Coalition of Labor Union Women
15 Union Square
New York, New York 10003

Interfaith Center on Corporate Responsibility
475 Riverside Drive, Room 556
New York, New York 10115

Corporate Data Exchange
198 Broadway, Room 706
New York, New York 10038

Institute for Food and Development Policy
2588 Mission Street
San Francisco, California 94110

Institute for Labor Education and Research
Center for Democratic Alternatives
853 Broadway, Room 2014
New York, New York 10003

Institute for Policy Studies
Project on Transnational Corporations
1901 Que Street, N.W.
Washington, D.C. 20009

North American Congress on Latin America
151 W. 19th Street, 9th Floor
New York, New York 10011

Pacific Studies Center
222B View Street
Mountain View, California 94041

Philippine Solidarity Network
707 Wisconsin Street
San Francisco, California 94107

Southeast Asia Resource Center
P.O. Box 4000-D
Berkeley, California 94704

Southeast Asia Resource Center
198 Broadway
New York, NY 10038

Southerners for Economic Justice
P.O. Box 240
Durham, North Carolina 27702

Women in the Eighties Project
Center for Investigative Reporting
54 Mint Street, Fourth Floor
San Francisco, California 94103

Women's International Resource Exchange
2700 Broadway, Room 7
New York, New York 10025

International

Center for the Progress of Peoples
48 Princess Margaret Road 1/F
Kowloon, Hong Kong

Christian Conference of Asia-Urban Rural Mission
2-3-18 Nishi-Waseda, Shinjuku-ku
Tokyo 160, Japan

Contemporary Archive on Latin America
Data Bank Project
1 Cambridge Terrace
London NW1 4JL, England

IDOC-International Documentation and
    Communication Center
Via Santa Maria dell'Anima 30
00186 Rome, Italy

Instituto Latinoamericana de Estudios
    Transnacionales
Apartado Postal 85-025
Mexico 20, D.F., Mexico

ISIS-Women's International Infor-
    mation and Communication Service
P.O. Box 50 (Cornavin)
1211 Geneva 2, Switzerland
and
Via Santa Maria dell'Anima 30
00186 Rome, Italy

Mexico-U.S. Border Program
Mexican Friends Service Committee
Ignacio Mariscal 132
Mexico 1, D.F., Mexico

Pacific-Asia Resources Center
P.O. Box 5250
Tokyo International, Japan

Transnational Institute
Feminism Project
Paulus Potterstraat 20
1071 DA Amsterdam, Netherlands

INTERVIEWS*

Linda Gail Arrigo	January 1983
Louis Berthold	June 1980
Michael Eisenscher	January 1983
Cynthia Enloe	January 1983
Rachel Grossman	April 1980
Rachel Grossman	March 1983
Bill Mitchell	March 1980
Charito Planas	June 1983

Gloria Scott   April 1980
Lenny Siegel   May 1980
Emmy Simmons   April 1980
State Department Official   April 1980

*Some of these interviews were conducted initially for "Women on the Global Assembly Line," *Ms.*, January 1981.

ABOUT THE AUTHORS

Annette Fuentes is currently doing research and writing on the status of women in countries around the world. She worked formerly at *Ms.* magazine and *Seven Days* and is a graduate of the State University of New York at Old Westbury.

Barbara Ehrenreich is a contributing editor of *Ms.*, editorial board member of *Social Policy* and fellow at the Institute for Policy Studies. She is coauthor, with Deirdre English, of *For Her Own Good: 150 Years of the Experts' Advice to Women.*

NOTE TO READERS

We encourage you to write to South End Press with your comments on pamphlet content, readability, design and, where appropriate, usefulness in your work.

The Institute for New Communications (INC) is a non-profit organization involved in popular education and media outreach to broaden public debate around political and economic alternatives.

INC Pamphlet No. 1
Poverty in the American Dream: Women and Children First
by Karin Stallard, Barbara Ehrenreich and Holly Sklar

Forthcoming Pamphlets
Plant Closures: Myths, Realities and Responses
Trilateralism, Reagan and the Neoliberals
Where Goes the Economy?
Jobs, Peace and Justice
Politics of Water
Food and Hunger in Urban America

Poster: *Who's Who in the Reagan Administration* by Holly Sklar and Robert Lawrence; a comprehensive, illustrated poster guide, 25x38 ($4.00 plus 50¢ postage).